Snapdragons

Stage 9

Gill Howell

Teaching Notes

Contents

Introduction

The *Snapdragons* series is a rich mix of different kinds of stories presented as picture books with expertly written text carefully levelled to provide reading practice at each stage in Key Stage 1.

This set of six books at Stage 9 provides a wide variety of genre including challenging, extended stories to encourage children to become confident readers. The stories have involved plots that reflect the feelings of the writer, with distinctive and rounded characters. The sustained reading required for these extended stories, with longer and more complex sentence structures, will help develop reading stamina. They also provide readers with further practice in reading key words, as well as widening their vocabulary through decoding specialised terms related to the different contexts.

The six books in Stage 9 include a variety of fantasy stories: a sci-fi tale, several humorous animal fantasy tales, a retelling of a traditional nursery story with a rhyming element and a new twist, as well as a traditional story from another culture.

While enjoying a sustained read with these longer texts, the children are still encouraged to look at the illustrations for visual cues to the words and to predict what is happening in the story. The picture book presentation will also inspire children to tell the story in their own words so that they develop their oral skills.

How to introduce the books

Before reading the story for guided or independent reading, always read the title and talk about the picture on the cover.

Go through the book together, looking at the pictures and talking about them. If there are context words (listed in the chart on page 4) that are new or unfamiliar, point them out and read them with the children. Read the story to the children, encouraging confident children to join in with you.

This booklet provides prompts and suggestions for using the books in groups and for guided, group and independent activities, matched to text, sentence and word level objectives. There are also separate Guided Reading Cards available for six titles at each stage. Suggestions are also provided for speaking and listening activities, writing activities, and cross-curricular links. You can use these suggestions to follow on from your reading or at another time.

Reading notes are also provided in each book. They can be found on the inside front and back covers of each book. These suggest friendly prompts and activities for parents or carers reading with their children at home.

Reading skills

Stage 9 develops:

- confident, independent reading
- awareness of more complex sentences
- understanding of a wider range of stories, beyond everyday experience
- awareness of more complex plots
- a readiness for conventional text layout
- inferential comprehension skills
- inferring author's intention
- awareness of other viewpoints
- insights into feelings and motives of characters
- consolidation of independent writing skills.

Vocabulary chart

Stage 9		
Alien Swap	Year 2 High frequency words	about after again an another as back be bed been but by call came can't could did do don't door down first from got had has have help(ing) her him his home how here if just last laugh(ed) little live love made make more much must name not now off old once one or out over push(ed) pull(ed) put ran school should so some take that their them then there these three time took two very want way were what when where will with would your
	Context words	stomach cabbage flying saucer alien laser wristband human mirror destination jacuzzi lunar
The Snow King	Year 2 High frequency words	about again an as be but by call(ed) came could did do door down first from good had have her here him his home house just last little live lived made man more must not off old once one out over ran saw seen sister so take that their then there time too tree two very way were what when will with would your
	Context words	daughter frozen wrinkled bundle bonfire delicious icicle
Molly and the Giant	Year 2 High frequency words	about after again an as back be because bed been but by called came could did do don't door down first from girl got had has help her here him his home house if jump(ed) laugh(ed) little live love make more much night not now off old once one our out over people pull put ran saw should sister so take than that their them then there these three too took two us very want way were what when there who will with would your
	Context words	castle giant enormous delicious palace magic sword purse
Mr Rabbit the Farmer	Year 2 High frequency words	again an as back be but called came can't could did do don't down from good had half have him his home how laugh(ed) little many more much not old one our out pull(ed) saw so some take than that them then there time too very way were what when where who will with would your
	Context words	crops vegetables fruit swede strawberries carrots cabbages neighbour barley beans thistles businessman harvest stalks wheat wheelbarrow sweetcorn
Hot Dog	Year 2 High frequency words	about after again an another back be because but by called came can't don't door down from good got had has have her here him his if jump(ed) just last laugh(ed) little love(d) make man more name next night not now off one or our out over people put ran seen some take that their them then there time too took us very want way were what when who will with would your
	Context words	meatballs traffic alleys restaurants hotel fairground museum
King Donal's Secret	Year 2 High frequency words	about after again another as back be because been but by called can't could did do don't door down first from girl good had has have her here him his how if just last laugh lived made make many may more must name next night not now off old once one or out over people pull(ed) saw seen should so take then that their them then there time too took us very want way were what when where who will with would your
	Context words	cottage forest nightingale donkey barber jail guards palace Your Highness prison

Curriculum coverage chart

Stage 9	Speaking and listening	Reading	Writing
Alien Swap			
NLS/SLL	Y2T3 23	T3, S6, W3, W6	T12
Scotland	Level A/B	Level A/B	Level A/B
N. Ireland	Activities: a, f, g Outcomes: a, b, c, d, e	Activities: a, b, c, e, f Outcomes: b, c, d, e, f, k	Outcomes: a, b, c, e, f, h, i
Wales	Range: 1 Skills: 1, 2, 3, 4, 5, 6	Range: 1, 2, 4, 5, 6 Skills: 1, 2	Range: 1, 2, 3, 7 Skills: 1, 3, 4, 5, 7, 8
The Snow King			
NLS/SLL	Y2T3 24	T3, S5, W3, W6	T10
Scotland	Level A/B	Level A/B	Level A/B
N. Ireland	Activities: a, b, c, Outcomes: b, c, d, e, i	Activities: a, b, c, e Outcomes: b, c, e, f	Outcomes: a, b, c, e, h, i
Wales	Range: 1, 2, 3, 5, 6 Skills: 1, 2, 4	Range: 1, 2, 4, 5, 6 Skills: 1, 2	Range: 1, 2, 3, 7 Skills: 1, 3, 4, 5, 7, 8
Molly and the Giant			
NLS/SLL	Y2T3 24	T3, S3, W7	T12
Scotland	Level A/B	Level A/B	Level A/B
N. Ireland	Activities: a, b, c Outcomes: a, b, c, d, i	Activities: a, b, c, e Outcomes: b, c, d, e, f, k	Outcomes: a, b, c, e, h, i
Wales	Range: 1, 2, 5 Skills: 1, 2, 3	Range: 1, 2, 4, 5, 6 Skills: 1, 2	Range: 1, 2, 3, 7 Skills: 1, 2, 3, 5, 7, 8
Mr Rabbit the Farmer			
NLS/SLL	Y2T3 24	T6, S1, W9	T12
Scotland	Level A/B	Level A/B	Level A/B
N. Ireland	Activities: a, b, c Outcomes: b, c, e	Activities: a, b Outcomes: b, c, d, k	Outcomes: a, b, c, f, h, i
Wales	Range: 1, 2, 3, 5 Skills: 1, 2, 3, 4	Range: 1, 2, 4, 5, 6 Skills: 1, 2	Range: 1, 2, 3 Skills: 1, 3, 4, 7, 8
Hot Dog			
NLS/SLL	Y2T3 23, 24	T3, S6, W10	T10
Scotland	Level A/B	Level A/B	Level A/B
N. Ireland	Activities: a, b, e, g, h Outcomes: a, b, c, d, f	Activities: a, b, c, e Outcomes: b, c, k	Outcomes: a, b, c, e, f, h, i
Wales	Range: 1, 2 Skills: 1, 2, 3	Range: 1, 2, 4, 5, 6 Skills: 1, 2	Range: 1, 2, 3, 5, 6 Skills: 1, 3, 5
King Donal's Secret			
NLS/SLL	Y2T3 24	T3, S7, W3	T12
Scotland	Level A/B	Level A/B	Level A/B
N. Ireland	Activities: a, b, c, g Outcomes: a, b, c	Activities: a, b, c Outcomes: b, c, d, e, f, k	Outcomes: a, b, c, e, f, h, i
Wales	Range: 1, 2, 5 Skills: 1, 2, 3, 4	Range: 1, 2, 4, 5, 6 Skills: 1, 2	Range: 1, 3, 7 Skills: 1, 3, 5, 7, 8

Alien Swap

Reading the story

Introducing the story

- Look together at the front cover, read the title and the author's name.
- Ask the children what the cover illustration shows, and to suggest what will happen to the boy and the alien in the story, using the title as a clue.
- Ask the children to look through the book briefly, focusing on the illustrations to confirm their ideas.
- Turn to pages 2 and 3. Ask the children to find the spoken words, and to read the words the author uses to describe how they are spoken (the reporting clauses: "he grumbled", "he whispered").
- Remind the children to use the reporting clauses to help them read dialogue with expression, rereading if necessary.

During reading

- Ask the children to read in a quiet voice as you listen to them individually.
- Praise the children when they read with confidence and self-correct on the run without prompting.
- On page 4, ask the children how the ellipses ("It's..., it's...,") help them read with expression.
- Where necessary, prompt the children to reread sentences and paragraphs to make sense of their reading.
- Encourage the children to make use of punctuation, and words used to describe speech in place of "said", in order to read expressively.

Observing Check that the children:

- respond to the punctuation while they read.

Group and independent reading activities

Text level work

Range humorous story/sci-fi/extended story

Objective To notice the difference between spoken and written forms through retelling known stories; compare oral versions with written text (T3).

- Ask children to take the role of either Harry or Zeto, and sit in the hot seat.
- Ask the role-players to describe what they did when they swapped places. Encourage children who take the role of Zeto to use their imagination to describe what they saw, and how they felt.
- Ask the other children to say what is different about the oral descriptions. Encourage them to think about the grammar in the first person recount.

Observing Are the children able to imagine themselves as the story characters, reading between the lines to imagine the characters' feelings and thoughts? Do the children understand the difference between a first person and a third person recount?

Sentence level work

Objective To turn statements into questions, learning a range of "wh" words typically used to open questions: "what, "where", "when", "who" and to add question marks (S6).

You will need question word cards: what, where, when, who.

- Give the group a set of the question cards, and place them face down.
- On pages 2–3, ask the children to read the first sentence and to pick out a question card. Model how to use the question card to make up one question about the sentence (e.g. "Harry glanced at the clock beside his bed": "What did Harry glance at?" "Where was the clock?" "Why did Harry glance beside his bed?" "Who glanced at the clock?")
- Encourage the children to read the remaining sentences and make up a question about each, writing it down and adding a question mark.
- Ask the children to read their questions aloud to a partner so that the partner can answer their questions orally.

Observing Do the children write their questions clearly and legibly with accurate punctuation?

Word level work

Objectives To discriminate, spell and read the phonemes "ear" (hear) and "ea" (head) (W3); To investigate words which have the same spelling patterns but different sounds (W6).

You will need white boards and pens

- Ask the children to turn to page 2 and put their finger on the word "tea".
- Write the vowels "ea" on the board. Ask the children to say the vowel sound in "tea" aloud.
- Ask the children to find the word "head" on page 5. Ask the children to say the vowel sound aloud. Ask: *Do the vowels sound the same?*
- Ask the children to search through the text and find any words with "ea" in them. Ask them to write the words with the short "ea" sound ("head") and the words with the long "ea" sound ("tea") in lists. ("hear", "please", "ear", "really", "meanwhile", "weakly", "teacher", "treat", "eat", "clean", "reason"; "breath", "breakfast", "unpleasant")
- Ask the children if they found any other words with the same vowel spelling, but a different sound. ("Earth", "learn", "idea", "great")

Observing Do the children scan the text to find the words? Are they able to hear the different vowel sounds?

Speaking and listening activities

Objective To work effectively in groups by ensuring each group member takes a turn, challenging, supporting and moving on (Y2T3 23).

- Ask the children one at a time to say what they liked most about the story.
- After each opinion is given, ask another child to agree or disagree, and to give his or her own opinion about the story.

Cross-curricular link

PSHE: take part in discussions with one person and the whole class

Writing

Objective To write simple evaluations of books read and discussed giving reasons (T12).

- Ask the children to write the title of the story.
- Let the children write a paragraph describing what they enjoyed most about the book (see Speaking and listening activity, above).
- Encourage the children to think of reasons to support their opinions, and to give evidence from the text.

The Snow King

Reading the story

Introducing the story

- Look together at the front cover, read the title and the author's name.
- Ask the children what the cover illustration shows, and to suggest what sort of story this will be.
- Read the opening of the first sentence on page 2 to the children, "Once, long ago in winter, in a cold, cold land..." and encourage the children to use the term "traditional tale" to describe this type of story.
- Ask the children to look through the book briefly, focusing on the illustrations to establish the story setting.
- Identify any new or difficult vocabulary for the children, e.g. "spluttered" (p8), "wrinkled" (p12), "icicle" (p24).

During reading

- Ask the children to read in a quiet voice as you listen to them individually.
- Praise the children when they read with confidence and self-correct on the run without prompting.
- On page 4, ask the children why the author has used "But" to begin the sentence describing Ivanka. (For emphasis.) Ask them how the effect would change if the word "But" was omitted.
- On page 6, ask the children to look for repeated words and phrases and suggest why the author has used them in this way.
- When the children find sentences beginning "And" (on pages 3, 5, 8, 18 and 24), ask them what effect these sentences have.
- Where necessary, prompt the children to reread sentences and paragraphs to make sense of their reading.
- Encourage the children to make use of punctuation to read in an expressive voice.

Observing Check that the children:

- use a range of strategies to work out new words.

Group and independent reading activities

Text level work

Range traditional story /from another culture/extended story

Objective To notice the difference between spoken and written forms through retelling known stories; compare oral versions with the written text (T3).

- Explain to the children that this is a traditional story, and how traditional stories and folk tales began by being told aloud.
- Ask the children to retell the story to a partner, and ask their partner to look through the book and comment on where the retelling differs from the written text.
- Encourage the children to think about how the text uses repeated words and phrases, then ask them to tell the story again.

Observing Are the children able to improve their retellings and use some rhythm and repetition for effect?

Sentence level work

Objective To write in clear sentences using capital letters and full stops accurately (S5).

You will need the following sentences written on the board:

but ivanka's heart was as cold as ice
the cold wind blew
katya did not feel afraid
when she awoke it was dark
go into the forest, ivanka
she froze to the spot

- Ask the children to rewrite the sentences, adding capital letters and full stops.
- Ask them to find the sentences in the text and check their own for accuracy.

Observing Do the children remember to use capital letters for names?

Word level work

Objectives To discriminate, spell and read the phonemes "ear" (hear) and "ea" (head) (W3); To investigate words which have the same spelling patterns but different sounds (W6).

- Write the vowels "ea" on the board and ask the children to suggest words that have these two vowels together in them. Write their suggestions on the board, grouped by their different vowel sounds.

- Ask the children to search the text and see how many words with different sounds they can find that have the "ea" spelling pattern. (1: near, cleaning, beaded, dreaming, eat, appeared; 2: earn; 3: great; 4: heart; 5: spread, heavy)
- Explain that "beautiful" has three vowels to make the sound, so it should not be included in their lists.
- Ask the children to read the words they found aloud and listen carefully to their vowel sounds.
- Ask the children to practise spelling these words using Look, Cover, Write and Check.

Observing Do the children scan the text to find the words? Are they able to hear the different vowel sounds?

Speaking and listening activities

Objective To present parts of traditional stories, own stories or work from different parts of the curriculum for members of their class (Y2T3 24).

- Ask the children to work in groups of four, each child taking the role of a character from the story.
- Encourage the children to work together to plan how to turn the story into a short play.
- Let the children rehearse their plays, then choose some groups to perform their play for the class.

Cross-curricular link

PSHE: take part in discussions with one person and the whole class

Writing

Objective To write sustained stories, using their knowledge of story elements: narrative, settings, characterisation, dialogue and the language of story (T10).

- Discuss the language used in typical traditional stories, and find examples of rhythm and repetition in "The Snow King" (e.g., pages 6 and 7, and 15).
- Suggest that the title of the story is changed, e.g. "The Rain King", "The Sun King" or similar, but the characters remain the same.
- Together, make notes of words and phrases that could be used for a new story. Ask the children to suggest how to describe the setting and the actions of the characters, using some repeated words or phrases.
- Ask the children to write a new story, modelling their language on the repetition in "The Snow King".

Molly and the Giant

Reading the story

Introducing the story

- Look together at the front cover, read the title and the author's name.
- Ask the children what the cover illustration shows, and to suggest what sort of story this will be.
- Ask them to look through the book briefly, focusing on the illustrations to confirm their ideas.
- Read the first sentence together on page 2, and ask what the first words, "Long, long ago" tell them about the sort of story it is. Encourage them to use the words "traditional tale".

During reading

- Ask the children to read in a quiet voice as you listen to them individually.
- Praise the children when they read with confidence and self-correct on the run without prompting.
- On page 5, read the sentence containing the dash: '"He loves children," she added, as she closed the door – and Molly noticed…' to illustrate how a dash means a pause.
- Encourage the children to make use of punctuation in order to read expressively.
- Ask the children to read the giant's words expressively. Ask: *How would a giant say that?*

Observing Check that the children:

- follow the text with their eyes and read in the correct order.

Group and independent reading activities

Text level work

Range new spin on traditional nursery tale/extended story

Objective To notice the difference between spoken and written forms through retelling known stories; compare oral versions with the written text (T3).

- Read page 2 together and find the phrase "as brave as a bear". Ask the children to scan the text to find two more similar phrases where an animal is used as a simile or comparison. (p7 "quick as a cat", p11 "fast as ferrets").

- Look together at page 15, and point out how the author uses "Now" to begin sentences, and explain how a traditional story uses language that is "conversational" in tone.
- Ask the children to work with a partner and retell the story to each other, using the illustrations as a stimulus, and using the above two examples of story language in their retellings.
- Ask the children to compare their versions with the written text and say how they differ.

Observing Do the children include story language from the text? Do they think of their own story language to include?

Sentence level work

Objective To use standard forms of verbs in speaking and writing, and to use the past tense consistently for narration (S3).

- Write the following verb phrases on the board: "there are", "there lives", "she has", "she is", "Dolly cries", "Molly says", "an old woman peers", "as she closes", "Molly takes", "they can".
- Explain that these are all present tense forms of past tense verbs that appear on pages 2, 3, 4, and 5 of the story.
- Ask the children to rewrite the phrases, putting the verbs into the past tense.
- Ask the children to check their answers against the text in the book.

Observing Are the children confident in their knowledge of irregular past tenses?

Word level work

Objective To spell words with common suffixes, e.g. "-ful", "-ly" (W7).

- Turn to page 24, and ask the children to find a word on the page that tells readers how everyone lives ever after. ("happily")
- Explain that "-ly" can be added to words that describe something, such as "happy", to tell readers how a thing is done or said.
- Ask the children to be word detectives and scan the text for words ending with "-ly" that tell readers how something is done. (p7 "politely", "grumpily"; p20 "angrily"; p22 "gently", "silently"; p24 "happily", "completely")
- Ask the children to practise spelling the words using Look, Cover, Write and Check.

Observing Do the children scan the text to find the words?

Speaking and listening activities

Objective To present parts of traditional stories, own stories or work from different parts of the curriculum for members of their own class (Y2T3 24).

- Ask the children to work with a partner.
- Ask the children to read pages 22–23 of the story, and to think how to present the events as a play.
- Encourage the children to think about the actions they should use so that an audience would know what was happening.
- Ask some of the children to perform their play for the rest of the class.

Cross-curricular link

PSHE: take part in discussions with one person and the whole class

Writing

Objective To write simple evaluations of books read and discussed giving reasons (T12).

- Ask the children to write a book review using the following headings:
  Title and author
  What the story is about
  What I like about it and why
  What I don't like about it and why
  Who would like this story

Mr Rabbit the Farmer

Reading the story

Introducing the story

- Look together at the front cover, read the title and the author's name.
- Ask the children what the words "retold by" tell them about the story.
- Look at the cover illustration with the children, and ask them to suggest where the story is set.
- Ask the children to look through the book briefly, focusing on the illustrations to establish the story setting.
- Identify any new or difficult vocabulary for the children, e.g. p3 "neighbour", p4 "equal", p5 "thistles", p7 "businessman".

During reading

- Ask the children to read in a quiet voice as you listen to them individually.
- Praise the children when they read with confidence and self-correct on the run without prompting.
- On page 2, ask the children: *What does Mr Bear do when he harvests the food?* Ensure they understand the meaning of "harvested".
- On page 4, ask: *Why did Mr Rabbit cut the carrot into pieces?*
- On page 7, point out that Mr Rabbit's questions do not have any "question words" in them. Ask the children how they know they are questions. Encourage the children to read them with appropriate expression.
- On page 11, if the children struggle with the word "wheelbarrow", cover the end of the word and ask them to read "wheel", then cover the beginning and ask them to read "barrow". Remind them to break long words into smaller chunks to help work them out.
- Where necessary, prompt the children to reread sentences and paragraphs to make sense of their reading.
- Encourage the children make use of punctuation to read in an expressive voice.

Observing Check that the children:

- use a range of strategies to work out new words.

Group and independent reading activities

Text level work

Range traditional story/humorous story

Objective To read, respond imaginatively, recommend and collect examples of humorous stories, extracts, poems (T6).

- Discuss the plot and characters in the story with the children.
- Write the names "Mr Bear" and "Mr Rabbit" on the board and ask the children to suggest words to describe their characters in the story.
- Ask the children to suggest words to describe the tricks Mr Rabbit plays, and Mr Bear's reaction to them.
- Ask: *What do you think of Mr Rabbit's actions? Are they clever? funny? mean?*
- Ask the children to give an example of how the author makes the story funny.
- Draw up a list of words and phrases to describe the story, for use in a later writing activity.

Observing Do the children support their opinions with evidence from the text?

Sentence level work

Objective To read text aloud with intonation and expression appropriate to the grammar and punctuation (S1).

- Ask the children to work with a partner and turn to pages 6 and 7.
- Let the children take the roles of Mr Bear and Mr Rabbit, and read the conversation between them.
- Encourage the children to think about Mr Bear's plan to trick Mr Rabbit while they are reading, and to read with expression.

Observing Do the children respond to the punctuation while reading?

Word level work

Objective To learn new words from reading linked to particular topics, to build individual collections of personal interest or significant words (W9).

- Ask the children to look at page 2, find the words "fruit" and "vegetables", and write the words as list headings on the whiteboard.

- Get the children to scan the rest of the text to find the names of crops, and to write them as lists under the correct headings.
- Ask the children which list is the longer, "fruit" or "vegetables".
- The children can add the words to their personal word banks.

Observing Do the children scan the text to find the words? Do they know which crops are fruit?

Speaking and listening activities

Objective To present parts of traditional stories, own stories or work from different parts of the curriculum for members of their class (Y2T3 24).

- Ask some of the children to sit in the hot seat, taking the role of Mr Rabbit.
- Ask the other children to imagine Mr Rabbit is being interviewed on television and they are news reporters.
- Ask the child role-playing Mr Rabbit to describe why and how he tricked Mr Bear.
- Encourage the other children to ask questions, using "how" and "why" to begin them.

Cross-curricular link

◀▶ Science: green plants – seeds grow into plants

Writing

Objective To write simple evaluations of books read and discussed giving reasons (T12).

- Refer the children to the words and phrases discussed and collected in the earlier Text level activity.
- Ask the children to write a paragraph describing the story that would encourage someone else to read it.

Hot Dog

Reading the story

Introducing the story

- Look together at the front cover, read the title and the author's name.
- Ask the children what the cover illustration shows, and to suggest what sort of story this will be, and who the main characters are.
- Encourage the children to look through the book briefly, focusing on the illustrations to establish the story setting.
- Identify any new or difficult vocabulary for the children, e.g. p2 "hustle", p9 "restaurants", p12 "straight", p19 "measures".

During reading

- Ask the children to read in a quiet voice as you listen to them individually.
- Praise the children when they read with pace and keep track of longer sentences and paragraphs.
- On page 2, ask the children what they think "the hustle and the bustle" means.
- On page 4, ask: *What effect does 'And' have? Does it make you pause more for emphasis?*
- On pages 8–9, tell the children to move the book to help them follow the swirling lines of text.
- Encourage the children to think about the characters as they read, and read their spoken words with appropriate expression. For example, ask: *How would Hot Dog say "NOW!" on page 12?*
- On page 19, check that the children understand what Hot Dog means when he says "Desperate times need desperate measures."

Observing Check that the children:

- read with confidence, only pausing to work out words briefly, and rereading to maintain comprehension of the sentence.

Group and independent reading activities

Text level work

Range humorous/extended story

Objective To notice the difference between spoken and written forms through retelling known stories; compare oral versions with the written text (T3).

- Ask the children to read pages 2–3 and to think about the different characters of Hot Dog, Mooch and Pooch. Ask them to describe these characters in their own words.
- Ask children to take turns to sit in the hot seat in the role of Hot Dog, Mooch or Pooch, and to describe the events of the story from their point of view.
- Ask the children to suggest how the story differs when told from another point of view.

Observing Are the children able to put themselves into the role of different characters? Do the children notice the difference in the grammar of their retellings, e.g. 1st person verbs?

Sentence level work

Objective To turn statements into questions, learning a range of "wh" words typically used to open questions: "what", "where", "when", "who" and to add question marks (S6).

- Write the following sentences from the story on the board:
  Hot Dog was a city dog.
  Mrs Fortini loved Hot Dog.
  Hot Dog and Mooch were waiting by her back door.
  Snatcher ran after them.
  They darted through the traffic.

- Write the following question words on the board: "what", "where", "who", "why", "when".
- Demonstrate how to turn the first sentence into a question, e.g. "Who was Hot Dog?"
- Ask the children to choose question words to turn each of the statements into questions, e.g. "Where did they dart?" "Who darted through the traffic?"

Observing Do the children write their questions clearly, beginning with capital letters and adding question marks?

Word level work

Objective To use synonyms and other alternative words/phrases that express same or similar meanings; to collect, discuss similarities and shades of meaning and use to extend and enhance writing (W10).

- On pages 8–9, ask the children to write down the verbs.
- Read the sentences aloud, replacing the verbs with "ran". Ask: *Why did the author use different ways of saying "ran" in these sentences?*

- Ask the children to add the verbs to their personal word banks for use in future writing.

Observing Do the children understand how choice of word can enhance their writing?

Speaking and listening activities

Objectives To work effectively in groups by ensuring each group member takes a turn, challenging, supporting and moving on (Y2T3 23); To present parts of traditional stories, own stories or work from different parts of the curriculum for members of their class (Y2T3 24).

- Ask some of the children to use the notes they made for a new story (see Writing activity below) to tell their story to the group or class.
- Ask the listeners to comment on the stories, suggesting what was good about them or how they could be improved.

Cross-curricular link

PHSE: realise that people and other living things have needs and they have responsibilities to meet them

Writing

Objective To write sustained stories, using their knowledge of story elements: narrative, settings, characterisation, dialogue and the language of story (T10).

- Discuss the plot and characters in the story with the children.
- Write a basic short outline on the board using the children's suggestions, e.g. "A dog catcher tries to catch 3 dogs. A lady helps them to escape."
- Explain to the children how the author has arranged the story. (The beginning introduces the characters and the setting, the middle describes how the dogs try to escape from the dog catcher, and the ending tells how they finally succeed.)
- Explain that the children are going to make notes for a new story, using the same plot and setting, but with new characters, such as three cats. Tell the children to make their notes using the headings: beginning, middle, ending.
- Ask some of the children to tell their stories aloud to the class using their notes to help them (see the Speaking and listening activity above).

King Donal's Secret

Reading the story

Introducing the story

- Look together at the front cover, read the title and the author's name.
- Ask the children what the cover illustration shows, and ask them to suggest what the secret referred to in the title might be.
- Let the children look through the book briefly, encouraging them to focus on the illustrations to identify the characters and setting of the story.
- Ask the children to read the first sentence of the story, and suggest what sort of story it is. (a traditional tale)
- Identify any new or difficult vocabulary for the children, e.g. p4 "embarrassed", p7 "Although", p9 "courage", p20 "listened".

During reading

- Ask the children to read in a quiet voice as you listen to them individually.
- Praise the children when they read with pace and keep track of longer sentences and paragraphs.
- On page 2, if children have difficulty with "nightingale", suggest they break the word into syllables and then blend the syllables together.
- On page 5, encourage the children to read the words in the speech marks expressively.
- On page 6, ask the children to say what they think "spread the word" means.
- On page 17, to ensure the children understand what they are reading, ask: *Why did the King ask everyone to leave?*
- Encourage the children to read the lords' words on pages 20–21 with appropriate expression.
- At the end of the story, ask the children to suggest how the King has changed.

Observing Check that the children:

- maintain their understanding of the story as they read.

Group and independent reading activities

Text level work

Range humorous/extended story

Objective To notice the difference between spoken and written forms through retelling known stories; compare oral versions with the written text (T3).

- Ask the children to work with a partner, and retell the story to each other using the illustrations as prompts.
- Encourage the children to say how their oral version of the story was different from the written text.
- Ask the children to suggest how each other's retelling could be improved, e.g. by using story language, by using a variety of connectives to link their story.

Observing Do the children use traditional story language in their retellings? Do they listen attentively to each other?

Sentence level work

Objective To compare a variety of forms of questions from texts, e.g. asking for help, asking the time, asking someone to be quiet (S7).

- Ask the children to turn to page 12, and find a question on the page. ("Can we stop here for a minute, Your Highness?")
- Write the question on the board and demonstrate how the question can be changed into a statement by altering the order of the verb (from "can we" to "we can").
- Ask the children to look through the rest of the text and find all the other questions.
- Ask them to say which questions cannot be turned into complete statements by altering the order of the verb. (Those beginning with question words – "What", "How" and "Why".)

Observing Do the children scan the text for question marks in order to identify the questions?

Word level work

Objective To discriminate, spell and read the phonemes "ear" (hear) and "ea" (head) (W3).

- Write the words "ear" and "head" on the board and remind the children how "ea" makes a different sound in each of these words.

- Ask the children to be word-detectives and to find all the examples of words with "ea" in them, up to page 15.
- Get the children to write the words on their boards, grouping them according to their vowel sounds. ("clearing", "fear", "ears", "please", "really", "year"; "head", "spread"; "heart")
- Ask the children to practise their spelling using Look, Cover, Write and Check.
- The children can add the words to their personal word banks for use in future writing.

Observing Do the children recognise that "year" and "heart" do not have the same vowel sound?

Speaking and listening activities

Objective To present parts of traditional stories, own stories or work from different parts of the curriculum for members of their class (Y2T3 24).

- Ask some children to sit in the hot seat, in the role of either King Donal or Morna.
- Ask the child to describe why Donal became glad he has big ears.
- Encourage others to ask Donal or Morna questions about the events, using "How" or "Why" to open their question.

Cross-curricular link

PHSE: identify and respect the differences and similarities between people

Writing

Objective To write simple evaluations of books read and discussed giving reasons (T12).

- Write the following headings on the board:
  - Title
  - Author
  - What the story is about
  - What I liked most about the story
- Who else would enjoy this story? Ask the children to use the headings to write a book review to encourage others to read this book.

Oxford Reading Tree resources at this level

There is a range of material available at a similar level to these stories which can be used for consolidation or extension.

Stage 9

Teacher support

- Teacher's Handbook
- Take-Home Card for each story
- Storytapes
- Woodpeckers Photocopy Masters
- Group Activity Sheets Book 3 Stages 6–9
- ORT Games Stages 6–9

Further reading

- Oxford Reading Tree Storybooks for Core Reading
- Woodpeckers Phonics Anthologies 2–5
- Playscripts Stages 6 & 7
- Fireflies Non-Fiction
- Fact Finders Units D and E
- Glow-worms Poetry

Electronic

- Clip Art
- Stage 6 & 7 Talking Stories
- ORT Online www.OxfordReadingTree.com
- Floppy and Friends

OXFORD
UNIVERSITY PRESS

Great Clarendon Street, Oxford OX2 6DP

Oxford University Press is a department of the University of Oxford. It furthers the University's objective of excellence in research, scholarship, and education by publishing worldwide in

Oxford New York

Auckland Bangkok Buenos Aires Cape Town Chennai Dar es Salaam Delhi Hong Kong Istanbul Karachi Kolkata Kuala Lumpur Madrid Melbourne Mexico City Mumbai Nairobi São Paulo Shanghai Taipei Tokyo Toronto

Oxford is a registered trade mark of Oxford University Press in the UK and in certain other countries

© Oxford University Press 2005

The moral rights of the author have been asserted

Database right Oxford University Press (maker)

First published 2005

All rights reserved. No part of this publication may be reproduced, stored in a retrieval system, or transmitted, in any form or by any means, without the prior permission in writing of Oxford University Press, or as expressly permitted by law, or under terms agreed with the appropriate reprographics rights organization. Enquiries concerning reproduction outside the scope of the above should be sent to the Rights Department, Oxford University Press, at the address above

You must not circulate this book in any other binding or cover and you must impose this same condition on any acquirer

British Library Cataloguing in Publication Data

Data available

Series adviser Shirley Bickler

Cover illustration Eric Smith

Teacher's Notes: ISBN 0 19 8455763

10 9 8 7 6 5 4 3 2 1

Page make-up by Fakenham Photosetting, Fakenham, Norfolk

Printed in Hong Kong